Media Literacy Workbook

Second Edition

Kimb Massey
San Jose State University

THOMSON

WADSWORTH

Australia • Canada • Mexico • Singapore • Spain • United Kingdom • United States

Printed in Canada
2   3   4   5   6   7   07   06   05

Printer: Transcontinental Printing/Louiseville

0-534-64394-9

For more information about our products, contact us at:
**Thomson Learning Academic Resource Center
1-800-423-0563**

For permission to use material from this text or product, submit a request online at
http://www.thomsonrights.com
Any additional questions about permissions can be submitted at
thomsonrights@thomson.com

Thomson Wadsworth
10 Davis Drive
Belmont, CA 94002-3098
USA

Asia
Thomson Learning
5 Shenton Way #01-01
UIC Building
Singapore 068808

Australia/New Zealand
Thomson Learning
102 Dodds Street
Southbank, Victoria 3006
Australia

Canada
Nelson
1120 Birchmount Road
Toronto, Ontario M1K 5G4
Canada

Europe/Middle East/South Africa
Thomson Learning
High Holborn House
50/51 Bedford Row
London WC1R 4LR
United Kingdom

Latin America
Thomson Learning
Seneca, 53
Colonia Polanco
11560 Mexico D.F.
Mexico

Spain/Portugal
Paraninfo
Calle/Magallanes, 25
28015 Madrid, Spain

Table of Contents

Introduction and Orientation

What is Media Literacy?

In the beginning, literacy was a word that described having knowledge of printed material (reading and writing letters or symbols.) However, these days, communication is flowing to and around us in a variety of forms besides print (e.g., radio, television, film, video games, photography, digital data, etc.) Media are such a crucial part of our contemporary society that most of us will spend more time interacting with media than doing just about anything else (even eating, sleeping or having conversations with other human beings.) When you stop to reflect upon the media and consider their influence on, for example, the incredible change our society is experiencing (major shifts in our politics, economic systems and cultural practices on a global scale) you become more aware of the deep inter-dependent relationship we have with media. A relationship that demands some serious attention and reflection because the resultant stakes are so high.

Recognizing that media are everywhere and presenting information about practically all subjects, it is no wonder that educators from various disciplines (media and otherwise) have sounded alarms and called for media literacy as a necessary skill-set for the public to have. The hope is that media literacy will empower the public, support the individual and positively effect the progress of culture and society. Media literacy's goal is to make the public active participants in the process of mass communication and the creation of meaning instead of pawns of the powerful mass communicators. But what exactly is meant by media literacy? What kinds of skills need to be learned?

In order to better understand media and become media literate, you must have a basic knowledge of mass communication because media are in the business of mass communicating. In the past, mass communication has been studied by breaking the process into its separate components: The basic communication model is presented this way:

A <u>source</u> sends a <u>message</u> through a <u>channel</u> to a <u>receiver</u> who provides <u>feedback</u>. At times there might be a problem completing the communication due to <u>noise</u> or <u>interference</u>.

These components make it easy to compare different types of communication. Consider the difference between interpersonal and mass communication in the model below:

	INTERPERSONAL COMMUNICATION	MASS COMMUNICATION
SOURCE	one or few people	corporation, group
MESSAGE	can be complex and specific	simple and general for maximum audience reach
CHANNEL	air, vocal chords, facial expressions	electronic distribution (sound and pictures)
RECEIVER	one or a few people	masses (large numbers of people)
FEEDBACK	instant and direct	delayed and indirect

What makes mass communication a significant phenomenon is the scope of its impact. Millions and millions of people receive a carefully and strategically formulated message at exactly the same time. That's powerful. The model above distinguishes mass communication from other types of communication—setting the stage for us to discover a concrete concept of media literacy.

Media literacy has been defined several different ways because media and mass communication have been studied from a variety of approaches. Interestingly, these approaches, too, can trace their roots back to the basic communication model. For example, in the past, some media researchers concentrated on the source component of the mass communication process. They proceeded with the idea that media effects are direct and audiences were passive or non-participatory. Other scholars have approached the content of media messages as a "text" worthy of evaluation regardless of the intent of the media producer (source) or the interpretation of the audience (receiver). Still a third group was more interested in media audiences (receivers) and their interpretations of messages.

However, some scholars have focused on the overall process of mass communication by analyzing the sum of all the parts while considering how they influence one another. To highlight a just a few approaches: Historians, for example, are concerned with the historical contexts or where and when media is created and consumed to illuminate when and how cultural meaning occurs. Cultural studies researchers are concerned with how media participate in the creation and maintenance of culture and political structures that, for example, might advantage some groups while disadvantaging others. While, gender scholars view media as an intricate part of the overall production of cultural meaning by its presentation of specific gender identities and politically motivated power structures as "appropriate or normal" or as "the way things are or should be."

Regardless of which context is used to view media literacy or which component of the mass communication process is highlighted, the consensus seems to be that it is important for people to become more media literate in order to improve media content and consequently the culture and the future. But how is media literacy achieved?

Media scholar Art Silverblatt provides one of the best overall definitions of media literacy. He writes, "Media literacy promotes the critical thinking skills that empower people to make independent judgements and informed decisions in response to information conveyed through the channels of mass communications" (1995, p. 2). He divides media literacy into five basic elements:

1. Being aware that media impact us on both the individual and societal levels. Because we live in such a media-rich environment, we are interacting with media and communication technologies (both consciously and unconsciously) throughout our everyday lives. Consequently, our perceptions (of the world and ourselves), our evaluations (of what is right and wrong) and our actions (what we choose to do) are closely tied with our relationship or interaction with media. By becoming aware of the role media play in our lives, we can better control their influence.

2. Understanding the process of mass communication.
This is equivalent to knowing "the rules of the game." If you are knowledgeable about the how media messages are produced, transmitted and interpreted, then you can be an active participant in (as opposed to a passive observer of) the process. In other words, the more involved we become in the mass communication process, the more we can shape our experience rather than have it shape us.

3. Developing strategies with which to analyze and discuss media messages.
Thousands if not millions of dollars go into the careful planning and creation of media messages. Audiences are analyzed, tastes are defined or created, communication is sharpened. Content is evaluated and re-evaluated to achieve the most efficient and effective communication possible. Why then would audience members simply consume or interpret media messages at face value? That would be a naïve way to respond to media content (but probably a reaction advertisers would relish). Having a strategy for analyzing the complex media messages and being able to debate their validity and value with others would make us more reflective and effective consumers of media.

4. Being aware that media texts can provide us with insight about who we are and about our culture. Media are the cultural storytellers of our time. When we look at the communication we create and consume (television, commercials, video games, computers, software, CDs) we can harvest clues about our culture by examining the presented values, thought processes, fears, attitudes, pleasures, lies, truths, etc. At the same time, understanding the culture better can also help us to more easily understand media messages.

5. Being able to enhance enjoyment, understanding, and appreciation of media content. Though you may choose to use your understanding and awareness as tools (weapons?) to deconstruct and criticize media, it isn't all bad news. Becoming a more aware consumer of media can also enhance the pleasurable parts of media interaction.

You will be able to enjoy media presentations on many different levels (from multiple points of access) and be an active participant in the meaning-making process.

Silverblatt has provided us with a simple roadmap to take us on our media literacy journey—one that is an ongoing endeavor with no final destination because media are constantly in a state of flux especially when new technologies are developed and introduced in the culture.

Media literacy is so important that many groups have been organized specifically to "take on the task" of researching the media and helping people become more media literate. The University of Oregon's Media Literacy Online Project (MLOP) lists nearly one hundred such literacy and education organizations (http://interact.uoregon.edu/MediaLit/mlr/organizations/list/).

The following exercises have been developed to give you an opportunity to consciously practice the media literacy skills set forth by Silverblatt. The topics and types of questions are varied. Therefore, they have been organized into categories by medium and subject so you can access them easily or use them in conjunction with other media texts.

Some of the questions will urge you to recognize and reflect upon your media consumption and interaction. Other questions will challenge you to step out of your usual media consumption to try something new. Finally, there will be questions that will require you to investigate a media "structured inequality" issue such as concentration of ownership, demographically targeted programming, or stereotyping.

As you proceed through this workbook, don't forget about Silverblatt's fifth element of media literacy. Media interaction can be pleasurable and insightful. And media literacy can lead to a better appreciation and enhanced enjoyment of what media have to offer. **So be sure to have some fun!**

Chapter 1: Media Literacy Concepts

Activity 1.1: Media Literacy Concepts

The Media Literacy Online Project (MLOP) presents eight key concepts for media literacy. Read and respond to each concept below. Explain your answer by providing an example that supports your decision.

1. All media are construction

The media do not present simple reflections of external reality. Rather, they present carefully crafted constructions that reflect many decisions and result from many determining factors. Media Literacy works towards deconstructing these constructions, taking them apart to show how they are made.

Do you think this statement is   TRUE   or   FALSE? (circle one).

Explain: _____

_____

2. The media construct reality

The media are responsible for the majority of the observations and experiences from which we build up our personal understandings of the world and how it works. Much of our view of reality is based on media messages that have been pre-constructed and have attitudes, interpretations and conclusions already built in. The media, to a great extent, give us our sense of reality.

Do you think this statement is   TRUE   or   FALSE? (circle one).

Explain: _____

_____

3. Audiences negotiate meaning in the media

The media provide us with much of the material upon which we build our picture of reality, and we all "negotiate" meaning according to individual factors: personal needs and anxieties, the pleasures or troubles of the day, racial and sexual attitudes, family and cultural background, and so forth.

Do you think this statement is   TRUE   or   FALSE? (circle one).

Explain: _____

_____

4. Media have commercial implications

Media Literacy aims to encourage an awareness of how the media are influenced by commercial considerations, and how these affect content, technique and distribution. Most media production is a business, and must therefore make a profit. Questions of ownership and control are central: a relatively small number of individuals control what we watch, read and hear in the media.

Do you think this statement is   TRUE   or   FALSE? (circle one).

Explain: _____

_____

5. Media contain ideological and value messages

All media products are advertising, in some sense, in that they proclaim values and ways of life. Explicitly or implicitly, the mainstream media convey ideological messages about such issues as the nature of the good life, the virtue of consumerism, the role of women, the acceptance of authority, and unquestioning patriotism.

Do you think this statement is   TRUE   or   FALSE? (circle one).
Explain: _____
_____

6. Media have social and political implications

The media have great influence on politics and on forming social change. Television can greatly influence the election of a national leader on the basis of image. The media involve us in concerns such as civil rights issues, famines in Africa, and the AIDS epidemic. They give us an intimate sense of national issues and global concerns, so that we become citizens of Marshall McLuhan's "Global Village."

Do you think this statement is   TRUE   or   FALSE? (circle one).
Explain: _____
_____

7. Form and content are closely related in the media

As Marshall McLuhan noted, each medium has its own grammar and codifies reality in its own particular way. Different media will report the same event, but create different impressions and messages.

Do you think this statement is   TRUE   or   FALSE? (circle one).
Explain: _____
_____

8. Each medium has a unique aesthetic form

Just as we notice the pleasing rhythms of certain pieces of poetry or prose, so we ought to be able to enjoy the pleasing forms and effects of the different media.

Do you think this statement is   TRUE   or   FALSE? (circle one).
Explain: _____
_____

Source: John Pungente, S.J. From Barry Duncan et al. *Media Literacy Resource Guide*, Ontario Ministry of Education, Toronto, ON. Canada, 1989.

Activity 1.2: Media Interaction
Part of Media Literacy is becoming more aware of your relationship with media. Monitor your media activity for one day. Note every time you interact with radio, television, newspapers, magazines, billboards, Internet, Web, video games, ads on cell phones or ATMs, etc. Then answer the following questions:

1. What percentage of time during your day to you estimate is spent interacting with media or media technology of some sort?

2. What type of content do you consume that might typically appear in more than one media format (e.g., sports on television and the sports section of the newspaper)? How does the coverage differ from one format to another? Is the information consistent? Why would you use more than one medium to reference the same information?

3. Do the media provide you with <u>all</u> the information you want? Is there anything missing from contemporary media coverage? Be specific with your answer and suggest which medium and category (i.e., television sports) to which you believe this missing information should be assigned or housed.

Activity 1.3: Get the Media Monkey Off Your Back

Sometimes the best way to find out how connected you are is to disconnect all together. Absence *may* make the heart grow fonder, though.

1. What is the maximum amount of time (consecutive days in your entire life) you have gone without consuming media of any kind? What were the circumstances surrounding that hiatus?

2. Try to avoid media of all kinds (especially television) for a week. If that is too long (shame on you), try three days minimum. Try to get someone else to go cold turkey with you; see what kind of response or cooperation you can get.

    Briefly describe your experience. Was it difficult to avoid media? Were others willing to avoid media with you? Were your interactions with others affected? If so, in what way? Did you feel you were missing something? Explain your answers.

Chapter 2: Books

Activity 2.1: Book Interaction

Even those people who don't think they are frequent book readers might be surprised to find out just how much they really do read. This exercise will help you identify your extent and type of interaction with books across time.

1. List your two favorite children's books (those you read when you were a child), then answer the questions about each one:

   Children's Book #1 title: _____

      Why you read it: _____

      Why you liked it: _____

   Children's Book #2 title: _____

      Why you read it: _____

      Why you liked it: _____

2. List your two favorite books (you've read as an adult), then answer the questions about each one:

   Book #1 title: _____

      Why you read it: _____

      Why you liked it: _____

   Book #2 title: _____

      Why you read it: _____

      Why you liked it: _____

3. Are there any books you think *everyone* should read? What are they and why?

4. Are there any books you feel *you should* read but you haven't yet? What are they and why?

Activity 2.2: Books of the Present and Future
Indeed books remain a popular contemporary medium. They come in many forms (printed and electronic) and their content is incorporated by other media.

1. Go to a bookstore, to the library or online and check one of the most recent "Best Sellers" lists (there are many different lists like this). Does it seem to you that just about *anyone* can get a book published? What criteria do you think are used to deem someone's ideas worthy of being published?

2. Books now appear in a form other than what we traditionally think of as a book. D-books (digital books) allow readers to download content onto computers or handhelds. E-books (electronic books) are devices that hold digital content but are designed to mimic the "look-and-feel" of the hardcopy, paper-page book. What do you think about the prospect of reading an electronic version of a book instead of the usual paper-paged, hardcopy version? What are the pros and cons of each product? What are the pros and cons of each reading experience?

Activity 2.3: The Glamorous Life of Books

As with most products, books exist inside an industry that chooses, promotes and distributes content based upon market viability.

1. Choose a well-known book that has been made into a movie (there are lots of them out there.) Trace the proliferation of the book by finding out as much of the following information as you can:

Book title: _____

Author: _____

Book published by: _____

Book distributed by: _____

Rights retained by: _____

Film title: _____

Produced by: _____

Distributed by: _____

Screenplay written by: _____

Directed By: _____

Website address: _____

Soundtrack: _____

Other products (Happy meals, t-shirts, video games, etc.): _____

_____

2. Obviously, book publishers use subsidiary rights to try to offset the large investments they make to publish books. Do you think this is a good thing or bad thing for books? Why or why not?

Chapter 3: Newspapers

Activity 3.1: Newspaper Interaction

Journalist/satirist Dave Barry writes, "Newspaper readership is declining like crazy. In fact, there's a good chance that nobody is reading my column." Indeed, readership is fluctuating as newspapers try to compete with so many other media for people's time and attention. What kind of a newspaper reader are you?

1. Do you regularly read a newspaper or e-newspaper? Which ones and why?

   a)_____

   Why?_____

   b)_____

   Why?_____

2. Which sections of the newspaper most interest you?
   a)_____

   Why?_____

   b)_____

   Why?_____

   c)_____

   Why?_____

3. What other resources do you use to access news and information <u>besides</u> newspapers? Why do you choose these sources over others?

Activity 3.2: The Purpose of Newspapers
The world of the newspapers is changing. The number of urban daily papers is falling, chains control 80% of circulation, and advertising dominates content (some estimate up to 65%).

1. What do you think the role of the newspaper is in our culture? Specifically address issues such as profit, providing information and cultural effects. Defend your answers.

2. Readership among younger people is down. The "solution" debate revolves around whether newspapers should give this group what they want in order to win their readership or whether newspapers should give this group what *they should want*. What do you think? Defend your answer.

Activity 3.3: Newspaper Accuracy And Context

Select a prominent news story and compare newspaper coverage of the event with coverage from at least two other media of your choice (radio, television, Internet, magazine, etc.) Try to obtain reports from the same day if possible.

1. Answer the basic journalistic questions for each of the media. See where your information is the same and where it is different:

Newspaper	Medium #2:	Medium#3:
Who?	Who?	Who?
What?	What?	What?
Where?	Where?	Where?
When?	When?	When?
Why?	Why?	Why?
How?	How?	How?

2. Then ask yourself the following more in-depth media literacy questions: Who owns the media companies you chose to evaluate? Which advertisers support these organizations and who is their target market?

Chapter 4: Magazines

Activity 4.1: Magazine Interaction

Magazines are the print industry's way of niche targeting to a specific audience demographic or taste public. Convergence of the magazine industry is manifest in a variety of ways. To name just a few: 1) magazines have become "digitized" (called e-zines or just "zines"); 2) the magazine format (top and side reference information) is utilized on many Web sites, some newspapers and even digital cable menus; 3) magazines are being published to support or supplement other media (gaming magazines, Soap Opera Digests, PC or Apple Magazines) and/or media celebrities (e.g., Oprah Magazine, and , Mary Kate and Ashley Olsen Magazine). Answer the following questions in order to investigate your interaction with magazines and zines:

1. Do you subscribe to any magazines? Which ones and why?

    a)_____

    Why?_____

    b)_____

    Why?_____

    c)_____

    Why?_____

2. Do you subscribe to any zines or electronic magazines? Which ones and why?

    a) _____

    Why?_____

    b)_____

    Why?_____

    c)_____

    Why?_____

3. Even if you are not a subscriber, which magazines have you read recently? What were the circumstances surrounding your encounters with these magazines (sitting in a dentist's office, at a friend's house, etc.)?

a)_____

b)_____

c)_____

d)_____

e)_____

4. Take a look at the magazines and zines you've listed above. Who are they trying to reach? List the audiences (some defining characteristics or demographics of those audiences) who are targeted by these publications. Do you see yourself "fitting in with" or "belonging to" these audience categories? Why or why not?

Activity 4.2: Targeting With Magazines
One of the selling points of magazines is that they can fill a niche or be targeted to a smaller, more specific audience groups as opposed to other more mainstream media.

1. Use the Internet or your library to find references. Locate what you would consider to be an "obscure" magazine. Then, fill in the following information:

   Magazine title: _____

   Published by: _____

   Purpose of publication: _____

   Target audience: _____

   Type of advertisements (if any): _____

   Other magazines for this category (competition?): _____

   _____

   Number of subscribers (if known): _____

   Available in print and online: _____

   Do you think this magazine (zine) is fulfilling a need for a particular target audience? Or do you think it is *creating* a need or *creating* a target audience with its content? Explain your answer.

Activity 4.3: Magazine vs. Zine

Choose a magazine that is published in print form as well as electronically online as a zine. Then answer the following questions.

1. Compare and contrast the content of both the print and electronic versions of the magazine. Explain why you think some content is altered while other content is simply reproduced exactly in both versions. Evaluate advertisements separately.

   Advertising content:

2. Find out which version of the magazine has the highest readership (call the publisher's 800 number or search online.) Why do you think this is the case?

3. If you were going to start a magazine, what kind would it be? Would it be in print form or electronic? Who would be your target audience? What kind of advertising would pay for it? Explain your answers.

Chapter 5: Recordings

Activity 5.1: Digital Music Exchange
Investigate the range of your interaction with the music industry.

1. List at least five ways music is distributed in our culture. Which methods/formats do you use most and why? Is digital "better" than analog (CD vs. records, for example) why or why not?

2. Recording companies are coming up with new ways to encrypt digital data in order to prevent people from unauthorized duplication. Have you used digital technology to preview or create your own collection of music (downloads, MP3s, burning CDs, etc.)? How do you feel about the copyright debate (piracy vs. sharing of musical files for free)?

Activity 5.2: Return of Napster

MP3s are MPEG standard audio files used especially for digitally transmitting music over the Internet. Napster was an online business that was, by court order, shut down because it was involved in the unauthorized exchange of copyrighted music. Now Napster has returned with, according to its Web site (napster.com), "extensive content agreements with the five major record labels, as well as hundreds of independents. Napster delivers access to the largest catalog of online music, with more than 500,000 tracks spanning all genres from Eminem to Miles Davis." In order to avoid copyright infringement, Napster now requires you to pay-as-you-go ($.99 per song, $9.95 per album).

1. List two arguments for and against the free exchange of music files.

   #1 For: _____

   #1 Against: _____

   #2 For: _____

   #2 Against: _____

2. Can you think of any ways the recording industry can accommodate the public's desire for more flexibility of choice versus obtaining profits from music sales?

Chapter 6 Radio
Activity 6.1: Know Your Radio Station
Choose your favorite radio station and test how it is serving your interests by researching the type of programming content it provides you.

1. Use a stop watch or a time piece with a second hand to monitor an hour of radio programming. Make a note of the content how much time (total) the station spends on each type of programming:

   NAME OF STATION: _____ FREQUENCY: _____

   FORMAT:_____

   TARGET AUDIENCE: _____

Programming type	Total Time
music (or talk if it is a talk-based format)	= _____
dj talk or announcements	= _____
advertisements	= _____
news	= _____
station promos (contests, etc.)	= _____

2. Are you satisfied with the division of programming you receive from your favorite station? What would you change to make your listening time better?

3. Who owns this station? Is it a media company? How many other broadcast/media businesses does this company own?

Activity 6.2: Commercial vs. Non-Commercial Radio
Locate and tune-in to your local public radio station, preferably one that is a NPR (National Public Radio) affiliate. You can also log-on to the Internet to hear a digital simulcast of NPR's broadcast (www.npr.org).

1. What kind of programming do you find on this station? How does the format differ from that of your favorite commercial broadcast station. If public radio stations are required to be commercial free, how are they funded? What are the similarities and differences between an underwriting spot and a commercial?

2. What other kind of programming does this radio station feature during times when NPR is not broadcasting? Would this type of programming "make it" on commercial broadcasting? Why or why not? Is there any other content you'd like to hear that is not currently broadcast on commercial or non-commercial radio? Explain your answers.

Chapter 7: Film/Movies and Video

Activity 7.1: Film Interaction

UNESCO (United Educational, Scientific and Cultural Organization established in the 1940s) estimates that approximately 2.2 billion films are stored in archives around the world. Film represents an important historical, cultural record that must be maintained and protected. According to UNESCO.ORG, "Until 1950 inherently unstable cellulose nitrate was used as the carrier for films. In addition to the deformation and distortion of information by chemical decomposition, this material burns explosively and cannot be extinguished. This is why there are strict regulations for the storage of nitrate films. Such instability has been the cause of the loss of 80% of world holdings up to 1930 and 50% of holdings from 1930-1950. In the race against incessant decay, film archives all over the world are striving to redeem what is left of historical cinematographic heritage by recopying."

1. Do you agree that films are important, historical records of our cultural heritage? Why or why not? How many films do you pay to see (at the theatre) each month? How many movies do you rent on tape or DVD? How many films have you seen in your entire life?

2. Are all films equally valuable as historical/cultural records? List at least five popular films you have seen (box office successes.) Then list five less-popular (perhaps non-mainstream) films you enjoyed. How is the content different in these films? What about their production quality? Marketing? Star power (actors/directors/producers?) Are certain types of films more culturally significant than others? Does popularity or revenue success have anything to do with a film's cultural/historical significance? Explain your answers.

Activity 7.2: American and Foreign Films

Review these lists and then answer the following questions:

Top 25 American Movies (Source: American Film Institute)	Top 25 Foreign Films (Source: foreignfilms.com)
1. Citizen Kane (1941)	1. 8 1/2 (1963)
2. Casablanca (1942)	2. Persona (1966)
3. The Godfather (1972)	3. Seven Samurai (1954)
4. Gone With the Wind (1939)	4. Wild Strawberries (1957)
5. Lawrence of Arabia (1962)	5. City of God (2002)
6. The Wizard of Oz (1939)	6. The Bicycle Thief (1948)
7. The Graduate (1967)	7. The Passion of Joan of Arc (1928)
8. On the Waterfront (1954)	8. Andrei Rublev (1966)
9. Schindler's List (1993)	9. Grand Illusion (1937)
10. Singin' in the Rain (1952)	10. Rashomon (1951)
11. It's a Wonderful Life (1946)	11. The 400 Blows (1959)
12. Sunset Boulevard (1950)	12. Fanny and Alexander (1982)
13. The Bridge on the River Kwai (1957)	13. Umberto D (1952)
14. Some Like it Hot (1959)	14. Nights of Cabiria (1957)
15. Star Wars (1977)	15. Cries and Whispers (1972)
16. All About Eve (1950)	16. The Seventh Seal (1956)
17. The African Queen (1951)	17. The Mirror (1974)
18. Psycho (1960)	18. La Dolce Vita (1960)
19. Chinatown (1974)	19. La Strada (1954)
20. One Flew Over the Cuckoo's Nest (1975)	20. Three Colors: Red (1994)
21. The Grapes of Wrath (1940)	21. Ran (1985)
22. 2001: A Space Odyssey (1968)	22. Throne of Blood (1957)
23. The Maltese Falcon (1941)	23. Aguirre, Wrath of God (1972)
24. Raging Bull (1980)	24. Los Olvidados (1950)
25. E.T. -- the Extra-Terrestrial (1982)	25. Stalker (1979)

1. What criteria were used in choosing which films would "make" the list? What criteria do *you* think should be used to determine whether a film is worthy of being listed as a top film of all time?

2. How many of the American films have you seen? Do you think they were worthy of making the top 25 list? Why or why not?

3. Have you seen as many films on the foreign list as on the American list? If so, how did you find out about these foreign films? If not, why don't you think you are as familiar with this list of films as you are the American list? Explain your answers.

Activity 7.3: Purpose of Film

What qualifies as a successful film? Would it be a film that earns big bucks at the box office (or a blockbuster)? Films that are critically acclaimed? Or perhaps films that eventually become classics because they reflect a historical moment, innovate a production technique or special effect, or create a new genre? What is the purpose of film? Consider these ideas as you answer the following questions.

1. What do you think the role or purpose of film is as a mass medium? Explain your answer. How would you define a "successful" film?

2. Where do you position yourself on the spectrum between thinking of film solely as a revenue source (industry product) and thinking of film as a valuable contribution to culture (by telling important stories)—value beyond the profit-making potential? Defend your position.

Chapter 8: Television

Activity 8.1: Television Interaction

New technology has allowed more competition to enter the television landscape. The Internet, DVDs, VHS, Video Games, etc. all compete for the amount of time we spend on media consumption for entertainment or leisure.

1. What is your favorite television program? Why do you like it? What other programs do you tend to watch frequently? Why?

2. How do you make choices about what to watch on television? Are you in control of your own TV viewing habits? Do you choose by program type? By network? By cast? Do you find you tend to watch the same types or similar programs, or are your viewing habits more diverse? Explain your answers.

3. How do you find out about new content on television? <u>From</u> television? Or do you seek out information from other sources? If so, what are those other sources? Are they associated with television producers/broadcasters in any way?

Activity 8.2: Audience Flow

Television broadcasters try to produce audience flow. That is, they program similar or consistent programming so audiences will tune in and stay tuned (no flipping) over the course of a viewing period. Programmers also use strategies to "hook" people into watching television in the first place.

1. Look at the program schedule for any commercial network or cable channel you watch. This schedule is very carefully thought out and organized to create and maintain audience flow. See if you can identify instances of the following programming strategies:

Tent-poling: Scheduling a strong program between two weak (or new) programs.
Hammocking: Scheduling a weak program between two strong programs.
Stripping: Scheduling the same program at the same time each day of the week.
Stunting: Scheduling special programs (hour-long episodes of programs, sharing characters between programs or featuring special guest stars) to thwart the competition's special feature.
Stacking or blocking: Scheduling several episodes of the same program back-to-back (marathons) or scheduling several strong similar-type programs in a row.
Bridging: The creative manipulation of a program's start time (e.g., five minutes *after* the hour) to try to keep the audience tuned in by having the previous program end after other programs have already begun.

2. Can you identify any other programming strategies on your television schedule?

Activity 8.3: Cable Interaction

Research indicates that most cable viewers consistently watch the same 7 or 8 channels instead of taking advantage of the wide variety of cable offerings. Is this the case for you?

1. One of the presumed advantages of cable is that it is able to "niche" program: create more specific content for particular groups instead of producing general content for the masses. Make a list of 5 cable channels you are familiar with that program a very specific format. List the target audience is for this content.

Channel: _____   Audience? _____

Channel: _____   Audience? _____

Channel: _____   Audience? _____

Channel: _____   Audience? _____

Channel: _____   Audience? _____

2. With so many choices available, how do you stay informed about program offerings on your cable network? How much preparation (if any) do you do to make the most of your television/cable viewing time?

3. Can you think of any content that is *not* found on cable? Why not?

Activity 8.4: You Can't Show That On Television

In Fall 2003, CBS produced a very expensive miniseries called, "The Reagans" that, was based upon the Presidency of Ronald Reagan and was scheduled to air during Fall "sweeps week" to help boost ratings. A few days before sweeps, CBS made the decision <u>not</u> to air the program stating, ""We believe it does not present a balanced portrayal of the Reagans for CBS and its audience."

Some say the network was bowing to political pressure. Conservative groups opposing the series claimed it was distorted and thought a negative portrayal would be in bad taste due to the fact that the former President was still living and in poor health. Media critics felt the program should be aired as scheduled—after all, it was not the first fictional portrayals of a real person ever produced. In addition, many felt CBS's decision set a bad precedent by allowing special interest groups to censor network content.

Ultimately, the series was cancelled on CBS but still aired on their cable sibling: Showtime. According to Jeff Chester, head of the Center for Digital Democracy (a communications lobbying group,) Showtime and CBS are both owned by Viacom. At the time the series was to air, Viacom was anxiously awaiting federal action on rules to restrict ownership of local TV stations. If these changes were not made, Viacom stood to lose millions of dollars. So, Chester argued, Viacom needed help from White House and Congressional Republicans who probably would not like seeing Reagan portrayed negatively.

Do you think the program should have been aired or not? Why or why not?

Why was it okay to air the series on cable but not on a broadcast television network? What's the difference?

Chapter 9: Digital Media and the Web

Activity 9.1: Digital Interaction

We now live in a digital world. It wasn't that long ago when only those people who worked for the government or large corporations had access to a computer (probably connected to a mainframe). Now computers and digital information (in one form or another) have saturated our culture and touch our daily lives in countless ways (online learning, banking, working, playing, communicating, etc.).

1. Consider the following areas where computers play a role in your life. Next to each item, describe whether you are comfortable having computers involved with that particular kind of personal information or service.

Medical Records: _____

Banking: _____

Voice Recognition: _____

Grocery Membership Cards (track spending): _____

Military Weaponry: _____

E-voting (electronic voting): _____

Video Surveillance: _____

Interactive Home Security:_____

Digital Photography: _____

Special Effects (video/film): _____

Distant Learning _____

2. Are there any areas (not listed above) where you think computer/digital technology should **never** be? Why or why not?

Activity 9.2: Email

Email continues to be one of the most widely used parts of the Internet. But there is a good and bad side to everything.

1. How is email different than face-to-face, interpersonal communication? How is it similar?

2. Identify at least five benefits of using email followed by five risks of using email. Based upon your experience, have you enjoyed any or all of the email benefits? Have you ever been stung by any of email's pitfalls? Should we simply except email's imperfections as "part of the deal?" How can email problems be overcome?

3. Email can be used in many ways beyond personal communication with friends and family (e.g., bulletin boards, news alerts, advertisements, education, etc.)? How do you use email? If you only use it for personal communication, why haven't you tried other services email provides?

Activity 9.3: The Web

When the Web was first introduced, many had high hopes that it would be a democratizing medium. Therefore, for example, an individual's Web site could be as accessible to the public as a giant corporations' site. Mass communication production would no longer be limited to well-funded conglomerates.

1. Identify at least five Web sites that are produced by individual's or small groups. What kind of information do these sites feature?

2. Have you ever purchased anything online? Why or why not? Can you think of any products that would not sell well online? Should certain products **never** be available for purchase online? Explain your answers.

Chapter 10: Advertising

Activity 10.1: Advertising Interaction

The statistics support the idea that Americans watch hundreds of thousands commercials over the course of a lifetime. What kind of effect could that be having on us as individuals and on our culture?

1. Watch an hour's worth of television programming (<u>not</u> a movie on a premium cable channel—don't cheat) and make a note of the commercials you view, their duration, and the products they are advertising. How many minutes worth of commercials were presented in one hour? Is that amount too little, just enough, or too much? Defend your answer.

2. Based upon the type of commercials that were shown, describe the target audience for this hour of television? Do you consider yourself a member of that target audience? Why or why not?

Activity 10.2: Ads, Ads Everywhere

One negative aspect of contemporary advertising is that our world is awash in it; ads can be found just about everywhere (called advertising *clutter*).

1. See how many advertisements you typically consume in a single day. List at least 20 places you encounter ads (it won't be difficult to find them, they are all around you.) How do you feel being surrounded by advertising? What is good about advertising? What is bad about it? Explain your answers.

2. Several years ago, advertisers Gary Betts and Malcolm Green, two London ad execs, met with NASA and announced plans to turn the moon into a giant billboard by projecting corporate logos onto the moon's surface using reflected sunlight from two large, umbrella-shaped mirrors. A debate ensued about *how* this feat could be accomplished most efficiently and economically. But what about *whether* it is appropriate to use the moon for advertising in the first place? Do you think it is okay to advertise on the moon? Are there any places you think it would be inappropriate for advertising to exist? Why or why not?

Activity 10.3 Non-Commercials

You may or may not be aware there are high-production quality <u>anti-consumer</u> ads that have been produced but do not get aired even with offers to pay the going rate for air time. Go online a view some of their print and video ads produced by Adbusters (<u>www.adbusters.org</u>).

1. Why don't networks agree to air these anti-consumer advertisements? They are of high production quality and Adbusters <u>is</u> willing to pay the going rate for airtime.

2. Broadcasters are licensed to "serve the public interest". Wouldn't it be in the public's interest to see alternative points of view regarding advertising and consumerism? Do you think it is right for networks to censor what we see especially in terms of advertising? Defend your answers.

Chapter 11 Public Relations

Activity 11.1: PR Interaction

Recently Arnold Schwarzenegger was elected Governor of the State of California. His political/PR campaign was closely watched all over the country if not all over the world.

1. The following list represents several "definitions of Arnold" that were presented by his PR team. Which of these positive definitions do you remember and what did you think about them at the time? Has your opinion changed since then?

Arnold as immigrant; an American success story
Then: _____
Now: _____

Arnold as athlete; Mr. Olympia and Bush Administration
Then: _____
Now: _____

Arnold as a successful businessman
Then: _____
Now: _____

Arnold as family man with wife and children
Then: _____
Now: _____

Arnold as next-generation Camelot hero (his wife is related to Kennedys)
Then: _____
Now: _____

Arnold as activist; government reformer (terminator)
Then: _____
Now: _____

2. How did Governor Schwarzenegger's PR team handle negative information—specifically the allegations of his womanizing as well as reports of his "secret meetings" with Enron executives?

Activity 11.2: PR Professionals Or Spinmeisters?

There are more Public Relations professionals employed in this country than there are journalists. Does this mean that there are more people "spinning" information than there are people researching and developing it?

"Between the incessant, all-pervasive demand for clever spin and exaggerated hype—and an increasingly complex and confusing media-controlled universe—many of our once dependable 'truth-tellers' have been transformed into compliant spinmeisters, if you will."

Cynthia L. Kemper in "Living in Spin"
Communication World, April 2001, v.18, i3 p6

1. This quote by Ms. Kemper expresses a negative view of Public Relations. Why do some people view PR as a negative type of communication?

2. Others view PR as using mass communication to increase awareness, credibility, appreciation and acceptance of a product, service or concept. Do you think PR can be a positive enterprise? If so, under what circumstances (be specific). If not, why not?

Activity 11.3: Prosocial PR

Research the recent "positive" anti-smoking public relations campaigns (articles, press releases, advertisement on radio or television, etc.) Several campaigns have been launched by tobacco companies as part of court settlements.

1. What kind of information is featured in these PR pieces? Which portions are most effective and what changes would you suggest that might improve the overall presentation? Explain your answers.

2. How do these PR message compare to similarly formatted advertisements? Explain your answer, give examples as evidence.

ews Media and Information

dia Effecting You

dia Literacy presents a list of five questions (Source: CML Media Kit—
g) you should ask when interacting with media and/or mediated
a media news presentation (television or radio program, newpaper or
magazine article, Web site) and use CML's questions for evaluation.

1. Who created this message?

2. What techniques are used to attract my attention?

3. How might different people understand this message differently from the way I do?

4. What lifestyles, values, and points of view are represented in *or* omitted from this message?

5. Why was this message sent?

Activity 12.2: Inside And Outside Points of View

George W. Bush made a State visit to Britain—the first State visit since 1918. A week before, The Independent UK (12/12/03), reported that U.S. officials wanted to keep protesters out of sight, demanding a rolling "exclusion zone" around the President. An anti-war group, Stop The War Coalition, said it had been told by the police that it would not be allowed to demonstrate in Parliament Square and Whitehall and had been told by British officials that American officials wanted a distance kept between Mr. Bush and protesters, for security reasons and to prevent their appearance in the same television shots.

Meanwhile American NPR radio reported (11/17/03) a brief interview with President Bush just two days before the visit to Britain. When the President was asked about the estimated tens of thousands British protesters waiting for him. President Bush responded, "No, not concerned at all. Glad to be going to a free country where people are allowed to protest. Not the least bit."

1. Obviously two different accounts are being presented here. Which one do you believe is true (or are they both versions of the truth?)

2. How can we avoid ethnocentrism in the news? Should American news media spend time presenting outsider (non-American) points of view? Should we care about how the world perceives us? Or do we have enough concerns domestically? Explain your answers.

Chapter 13 Mass Media and Social Issues

Activity 13.1: Negative Stereotypes
Negative stereotypes can emerge in a variety of settings: race, gender, age, socio-economic status, religion, etc.

1. Pay attention to your television viewing for a day. Or think about some of the programs you usually watch. List any stereotypes you see (whether meant to be comedic or not). Be sure to pay close attention to <u>all</u> types of programming (commercials, public service announcements, news, etc.)

2. What would be a positive solution to counteract the negative stereotypes you listed in question #1? Is it better to <u>not</u> be represented in the media at all rather than be represented negatively? Explain your answer.

3. In your opinion, what are the long-term effects of negative stereotyping?

Activity 13.2: Theorist Name Dropping
A good place to begin learning about media effects is to study media theory and/or locating the experts: the media theorists.

1. Go online and locate the names of three contemporary media theorists. What aspect of media do they study (i.e., what are they "famous" for)? Where did they publish their research?

Theorist #1_____

   Topic:_____

   Publication:_____

Theorist #2_____

   Topic:_____

   Publication:_____

Theorist #3_____

   Topic:_____

   Publication:_____

2. There is a fun Web site that has created profile cards (in the form of baseball trading cards) for many of the more famous cultural theorists many of whom write about media. Check it out: www.theorycards.org.uk

Activity 13.3: Applying Theory

A good way to become more familiar with theories is to apply different ones to the same media interaction. That way, you can see the effectiveness and limitations of a particular theory.

Choose two of the better known mass media theories (e.g., Mass Society, Bullet Theory, Two-Step Flow Theory, Attitude Change Theory, Reinforcement Theory, Uses and Gratifications Theory, Agenda Setting Theory, Dependency Theory, Social Cognitive Theory, Symbolic Interaction Theory, Social Construction of Reality Theory, Cultivation Analysis Theory, Critical Cultural Theory, Feminist Theory, etc.).

1. Briefly describe each theoretical perspective and then apply them to a media encounter you have had recently (watching a television program, listening to the radio, etc.)

2. From this theory application exercise, what did you learn about your media encounter? What did you learn about each theory (strengths and weaknesses)?

Chapter 14: Media, Policy, Law, and Regulation

Activity 14.1: Censorship

Though laws do exist about what types of information [text obscured] Amendment and <u>can</u> be presented by media, there is [text obscured] (obscenity and profanity, for example).

1. Do you think media content should be censored i[text obscured] so, under what circumstances or what kind of inform[text obscured] [b]e allowed? Defend your answers.

2. Have you ever encountered media content that offended you (by the way offensive content <u>is protected</u> by the First Amendment)? If so, what was it? Have you been in a circumstance where others found content offensive, but you did not? Describe that experience.

Activity 14.2: The Federal Communication Commission

The governing body of media is the FCC. This exercise will help you get to know the Commission and its members better. Go online to (www.fcc.gov) for more information.

1. How many FCC commissioners are there? What are their names? How long have they served?

2. How did they become FCC Commissioners (were they elected or appointed?)

3. What kind of media experience are the Commissioners required to have? Should they have extensive media backgrounds in order to be Commissioners? Why or why not?

4. What upcoming legislation will the FCC be addressing in the near future?

Chapter 15: Media Ethics

Activity 15.1: Personal Ethics

Most everyone follows some sort of personal code of ethics—rules you live your life by or "lines" you will not cross.

1. What are some rules you keep (or try not to break) in the conduct of your daily life? Under what circumstances would these rules change (or be bent or broken?) Where did you learn these rules?

2. Do you keep separate sets of rules? That is, do you behave one way at home, another at work, and another in front of your parents or your boss? How do you rationalize these changes or the implementation of "situational ethics"?

3. Do you believe media producers should follow a strict code of ethics (like doctors or lawyers)? Why or why not? What should happen if the media break ethical rules (for example, printing a story that is not true)? How can the media be held accountable for their ethical behavior?

Activity 15.2: Ethical Codes

The American Society of Newspaper Editors (ASNE) recently reviewed 33 codes of ethics forwarded by their member newspapers across the country. ASNE then asked two leading thinkers, Bob Steele and Jay Black, to analyze these codes and "highlight the most common — and useful — ingredients of these documents to help editors evaluate their own codes, if they have one, or help editors create one, if they choose" (source: www.asne.org).

They wrote:

It's no surprise that the 33 codes of ethics offered by ASNE member newspapers include a wide range of approaches for handling moral dilemmas. Some are heavy on time-honored tradition and others venture into the impact of the new technologies at the turn of the new century...

The most popular subject in these codes is conflicts of interest to include a wide range of issues from gifts and junkets to political involvement and community activity. About half of the codes we examined dealt with the subjects of sources and matters of manipulation of photographs. Fewer still dealt with corrections and plagiarism.

Missing from many codes were standards or discussion of privacy, deception, identification of juvenile suspects and racial stereotyping. Fewer than one in five codes addressed the subject of editorial and advertising department tensions. Many codes ignored the subject of enforcement.

1. Review any media code of ethics. List three rules in the code. Do you think the rules are necessary? What happens if these rules are broken? What rules do you think should be added (if any) to the ethical code? Why?

Chapter 16: Globalization of Communications Media

Activity 16.1: Defining Global

How can you tell whether a country is <u>successfully</u> "global"?

In his article, "Getting Global," David R. Sands uses several criteria to determine the "global-ness" of a country: "trade as a percentage of gross domestic economy, percentage of the population using the Internet, foreign direct investment and the number of minutes of international phone calls per capita. While the United States scored highest among the top 20 countries in terms of technological innovation and the Internet, other countries ranked far higher in their interactions with the global economy and the exposure of their citizens to those outside the country" (<u>Insight on the News</u>, Feb 26, 2001 v17 i8 p33).

1. Do you agree that these categories should be the indicators? Are there any criteria you would add to or take away from the list? Defend your decision.

2. Why is it important for a country to "go" global or be perceived as "global"? What is gained by this activity? And what could be possibly lost?

Activity 16.2: Importing and Exporting Media Content

The United States is one of the biggest exporters of media content in the world. Some view globalization of goods and media as cultural imperialism. There are several countries (i.e., France, Canada, China, etc.) that have created legislation to limit the amount of imported content in order to slow down the dilution of their native culture.

1. What non-American media content have you consumed lately ("foreign" films, books written by a non-American authors or published abroad, an Australian Web site, etc.) What do you think about having access to this type of content? Do you see it as diversifying or homogenizing our American culture?

2. What about the reverse situation? Can you identify with other countries <u>not</u> wanting their cultures to become "Americanized"?

3. What would be a winning solution to the diversification vs. homogenization debate? How much and what kind of media content should be freely traded globally?

Activity 16.3: War In Iraq

War coverage is difficult because, on the most basic level, journalists must balance the people's right to know against information that might risk security. Of course, there are a myriad of other complexities to documenting and reporting war information.

1. What are some of the issues that have emerged from the Iraq War Coverage? How much access do you think journalists should have? Do you think journalists should <u>ever</u> be censored in their reporting? If so, under what circumstances? If not, why not?

2. Why has the reporting of Al-Jazeera been important during this War? What do you know about this network? Check out an English-version of Al-Jazeera (English.aljazeera.net) and compare/contrast its content to any American major newspaper. What stories are featured in each? What is the emphasis of each?